A PENNY

By ALLAN MOREY
Illustrations by JENNIFER BOWER
Music by JOSEPH FAISON IV

CANTATA
LEARNING

WWW.CANTATALEARNING.COM

CANTATA LEARNING

Published by Cantata Learning
1710 Roe Crest Drive
North Mankato, MN 56003
www.cantatalearning.com

Library of Congress Cataloging-in-Publication Data
Names: Morey, Allan, author. | Bower, Jennifer, 1969– illustrator. | Faison,
    Joseph, IV, composer.
Title: A penny / by Allan Morey ; illustrated by Jennifer Bower ; music by
    Joseph Faison IV.
Description: North Mankato, MN : Cantata Learning, [2018] | Series: Money
    values | Audience: Ages 6–9. | Audience: K to grade 3. | Includes
    bibliographical references.
Identifiers: LCCN 2017017500 (print) | LCCN 2017036113 (ebook) | ISBN
    9781684101665 (ebook) | ISBN 9781684101207 (hardcover : alk. paper)
Subjects: LCSH: Cent--Juvenile literature. | Coins, American--Juvenile
    literature. | Money--Juvenile literature. | Children's songs, English.
Classification: LCC CJ1836 (ebook) | LCC CJ1836 .M68 2018 (print) | DDC
    332.4--dc23
LC record available at https://lccn.loc.gov/2017017500

Book design and art direction, Tim Palin Creative
Editorial direction, Kellie M. Hultgren
Music direction, Elizabeth Draper
Music arranged and produced by Joseph Faison IV

Printed in the United States of America in North Mankato, Minnesota.
122017   0378CGS18

ACCESS THE MUSIC!
SCAN CODE WITH MOBILE APP
CANTATALEARNING.COM

TIPS TO SUPPORT LITERACY AT HOME

WHY READING AND SINGING WITH YOUR CHILD IS SO IMPORTANT

Daily reading with your child leads to increased academic achievement. Music and songs, specifically rhyming songs, are a fun and easy way to build early literacy and language development. Music skills correlate significantly with both phonological awareness and reading development. Singing helps build vocabulary and speech development. And reading and appreciating music together is a wonderful way to strengthen your relationship.

READ AND SING EVERY DAY!

TIPS FOR USING CANTATA LEARNING BOOKS AND SONGS DURING YOUR DAILY STORY TIME

1. As you sing and read, point out the different words on the page that rhyme. Suggest other words that rhyme.

2. Memorize simple rhymes such as Itsy Bitsy Spider and sing them together. This encourages comprehension skills and early literacy skills.

3. Use the questions in the back of each book to guide your singing and storytelling.

4. Read the included sheet music with your child while you listen to the song. How do the music notes correlate to the words of the song?

5. Sing along on the go and at home. Access music by scanning the QR code on each Cantata book, or by using the included CD. You can also stream or download the music for free to your computer, smartphone, or mobile device.

Devoting time to daily reading shows that you are available for your child. Together, you are building language, literacy, and listening skills.

Have fun reading and singing!

Pennies are one of the many kinds of coins people use for money. The front of a penny has a picture of the sixteenth president of the United States, Abraham Lincoln. Different pictures appear on the backs of pennies. Since 2010, the **Union Shield** is on the back of many new pennies.

A penny is worth one **cent**. To learn more about the value of coins, turn the page and sing along!

I found a penny,
and I picked it up.

It's worth one cent.
That's not that much.

A penny is worth just one cent.
A penny is worth just one cent.

I found a penny,
and it's coppery.

But other coins
are all silvery.

50¢ PENNIES

$5 DIMES

A penny is worth just one cent.
A penny is worth just one cent.

9

I found a penny.
My penny is round.

Watch it go rolling
across the ground.

A penny is worth just one cent.
A penny is worth just one cent.

I found a penny.
The **edge** is smooth.

Coins are all different,
and that's the truth!

HOW TO EARN

MONEY

HOMEWORK — 25¢

CLEAN ROOM — $1.00

— 50¢

READ BO — $1.25

BRUSH TEE — 10¢

CLEAR T — 50¢

TAKE OUT

SAVINGS

A penny is worth just one cent.
A penny is worth just one cent.

I found a penny.
It's just one cent.

It shows Abe Lincoln,
the sixteenth president.

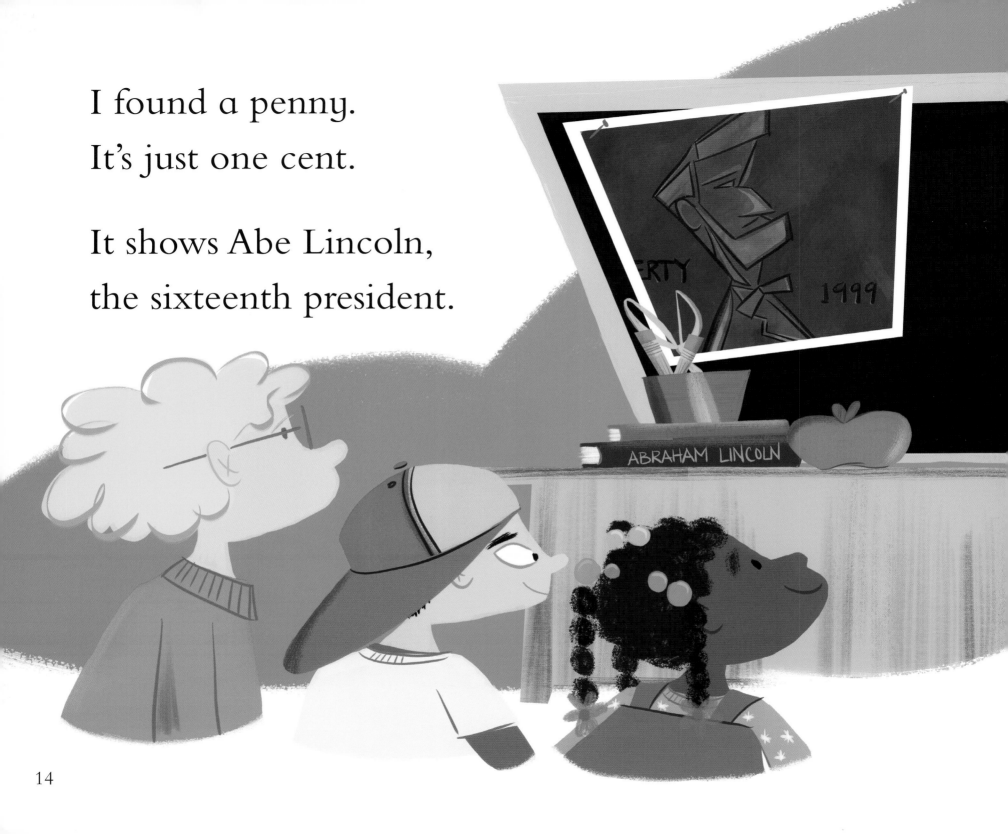

A penny is worth just one cent.

A penny is worth just one cent.

I found a penny. It's worth one cent.

The other coins are worth more in cents.

One thick nickel is five cents.

That's a pile of five pennies

One shiny dime is ten cents.

That's a stack of ten pennies.

One large quarter is twenty-five cents.

That's a leaning, tipsy tower of twenty-five pennies.

I found a penny
and ninety-nine more.

One hundred pennies
equals one dollar!

A penny is worth just one cent.
A penny is worth just one cent.

I found a penny,
and I picked it up.

It's worth one cent.
That's not that much.

A penny is worth just one cent.

A penny is worth just one cent.

SONG LYRICS
A Penny

I found a penny,
and I picked it up.
It's worth one cent.
That's not that much.

A penny is worth just one cent.
A penny is worth just one cent.

I found a penny,
and it's coppery.
But other coins
are all silvery.

A penny is worth just one cent.
A penny is worth just one cent.

I found a penny.
My penny is round.
Watch it go rolling
across the ground.

A penny is worth just one cent.
A penny is worth just one cent.

I found a penny.
The edge is smooth.
Coins are all different,
and that's the truth!

A penny is worth just one cent.
A penny is worth just one cent.

I found a penny.
It's just one cent.
It shows Abe Lincoln,
the sixteenth president.

A penny is worth just one cent.
A penny is worth just one cent.

I found a penny. It's worth one cent.
The other coins are worth more in
    cents.

One thick nickel is five cents.
That's a pile of five pennies

One shiny dime is ten cents.
That's a stack of ten pennies.

One large quarter is twenty-five
    cents.
That's a leaning, tipsy tower of
    twenty-five pennies.

I found a penny
and ninety-nine more.
One hundred pennies
equals one dollar!

A penny is worth just one cent.
A penny is worth just one cent.

I found a penny,
and I picked it up.
It's worth one cent.
That's not that much.

A penny is worth just one cent.
A penny is worth just one cent.

A Penny

Jazz/New Orleans Second Line
Joseph Faison IV

Verse

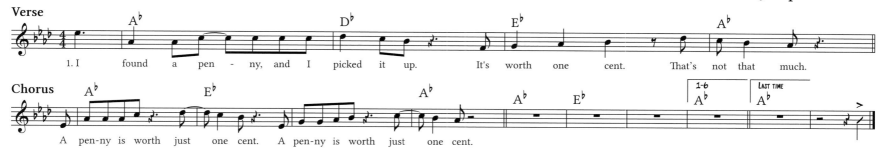

1. I found a pen-ny, and I picked it up. It's worth one cent. That's not that much.

Chorus

A pen-ny is worth just one cent. A pen-ny is worth just one cent.

Verse 2
I found a penny, and it's coppery.
But other coins are all silvery.

Chorus

Verse 3
I found a penny. My penny is round.
Watch it go rolling across the ground.

Chorus

Verse 4
I found a penny. The edge is smooth.
Coins are all different, and that's the truth!

Chorus

Verse 5
I found a penny. It's just one cent.
It shows Abe Lincoln, the sixteenth president.

Chorus

Verse 6
I found a penny. It's worth one cent.
The other coins are worth more in cents.

Bridge

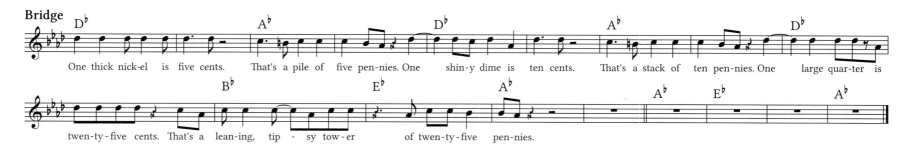

One thick nick-el is five cents. That's a pile of five pen-nies. One shin-y dime is ten cents. That's a stack of ten pen-nies. One large quar-ter is twen-ty-five cents. That's a lean-ing, tip-sy tow-er of twen-ty-five pen-nies.

Verse 7
I found a penny and ninety-nine more.
One hundred pennies equals one dollar!

Chorus

Verse 8
I found a penny, and I picked it up.
It's worth one cent. That's not that much.

Chorus

GLOSSARY

cent—the smallest unit of money in the United States

edge—the thin outer side of a coin

Union Shield—a symbol from the Civil War that represents how Abraham Lincoln fought to keep the nation together. On the shield are thirteen stripes, for the original thirteen colonies. Also on the back is the motto of the United States, "E Pluribus Unum" or "Out of many, one." This saying means that out of many states we have one strong nation.

GUIDED READING ACTIVITIES

1. Grab some coins to practice what you learned on pages 16 and 17. Find a nickel and count out how many pennies are equal to one nickel. Then find a dime and count out how many pennies equal one dime. Next, do this for a quarter.

2. Sort your pennies into piles with the same picture on the back.

3. One hundred pennies equals one dollar. But how many nickels equal a dollar? How many dimes make a dollar? How many quarters?

TO LEARN MORE

Cleary, Brian P. *A Dollar, a Penny, How Much and How Many?* Minneapolis: Millbrook, 2012.

Deen, Marilyn. *Dollars and Cents*. North Mankato, MN. Capstone, 2012.

Edison, Erin. *Abraham Lincoln*. North Mankato, MN: Capstone, 2013.

Morey, Allan. *A Nickel*. North Mankato, MN: Cantata Learning, 2018.